Nectarine Nonsense

Nina Cairo

Nectarine Nonsense

ISBN: 979-8-8689-2160-5 (Paperback)

Library of Congress Control Number: 2024924403

Cover design by Nina Cairo.

First edition: 2024

Preface

I wrote my earliest recorded poem as a seven-year-old in my sparkly rainbow, peace sign, star, and heart-covered notebook. This lively journal completely juxtaposes the poem I am about to share, which represents the duality of being human: we are sparkly rainbow notebooks and sad, dark poems all at once.

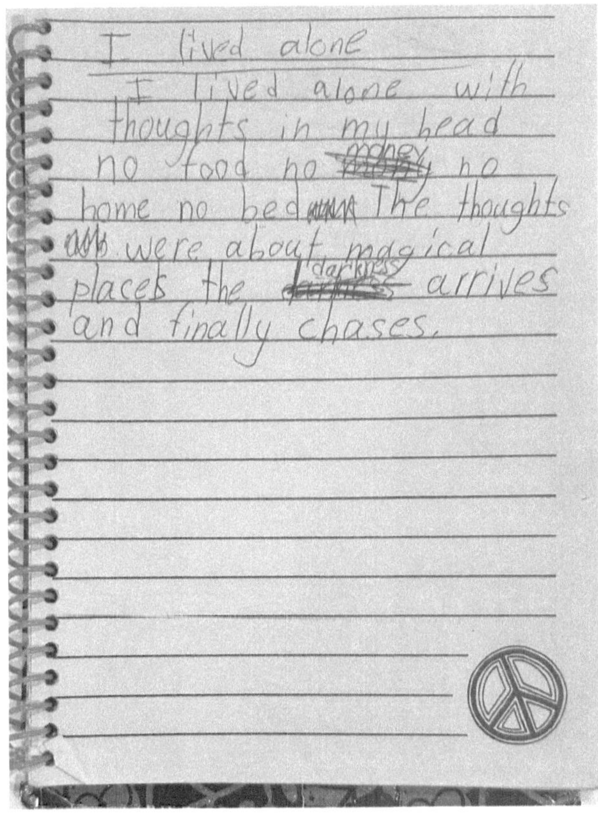

After finishing my poem, I eagerly showed it to my friends and teacher, who returned horrified looks. They didn't understand why a seven-year-old would write such an eerie poem. I have teetered along the line of darkness since I was four, but I have always found the light through poetry. Poetry has allowed me to unleash the tangled mess of thoughts in my head, understand complicated emotions, and serve up life situations with a side of wordplay.

I've been collecting pieces of my life for a few years, crafting them into the poems in this book. Some of these poems are pleasant, and most of them are somber. However, even the poems written during dark times led to a positive change in my life. I will keep growing through poetry. It is a living, breathing force that will surely be with me for the rest of my days.

Contents

Skin:

The wounded and bruised layer that affects the whole fruit; dealing with disorders and mental health struggles.

Marbles

I've lost my marbles
like I've lost my smile.
They rolled into the darkness,
into a sea of denial.

Maybe they're in the corner
at which I stare.
Or floating in my tears,
coming up for air.

Maybe they're under the floorboards
on the ground where I rest.
Or nestled up tight
in the hole in my chest.

Maybe they're with
the dominoes and jacks.
Oh, where are my marbles,
and when will they come back?

Body Heat

My back is a stovetop,
and my face is a furnace.
Every goosebump and hair
stings like a fire poker.
The hallucinogenic heat of mid-July
lurks over me.
I can feel myself rising
and boiling and simmering.

Worst Enemy

You push me down
and make me frown
at every chance you get.

With whispers in my ear,
you make me fear
when things haven't happened yet.

In exhaustion, I sigh,
then proceed to cry
until you take away my air.

I have to succeed
for your accomplishment greed,
which I don't think is fair.

But now I see

that you are me,

and I am my worst enemy.

Mind Matter

My mind was a sweater flipped and twisted inside
out-
side, frontside, backside, all sides
twisted all wrong.
A wad of chaos.
Arms flailing, trying to unwind.

Brain was a battlefield.
Thoughts fighting me,
me fighting back,
back burning with hot fear,
steaming anxiety,
burning disaster,
sweltering obsession.

Why am I the way I am?
Who am I really
if there are two parts of me?
One begging for normalcy.
One poisoning with negativity.

I know the dark side of the moon
and the deep ocean floor.
I know the ground beneath my feet
that I've stared at for so long
as I repeat, "It's okay,"s and
"that's not true"s back at my mind.

I reached the light at the end of the tunnel,
but I can't forget the journey through.
The shadows that followed me there

still linger.
But now I turn around
and stare them down.

I bask in the moonlight.
I float to the top of the sea.
But I can never forget
the things that haunted me.

City Mindset

My mind is as loud as a city
with traffic in every vessel.
Honks and yelling voices
ricochet in every direction.
It's trapped in constant inertia
and a never-ending frenzy.
The rumble of a million steps
causes a tumultuous disruption.
I'm exhausted and overwhelmed.
I need a moment of stillness.

Remembering Rings

I stare at the cup rings on my nightstand.
They are prehistoric reminders of what was once
there:
memories of a thirst quenched,
a body fulfilled and nourished,
and a soul willing to replenish itself.
The wood of stability has been altered,
permanently marked by circles of stagnancy.

I Might

I might change my sheets today.
I might take my dirty cups to the kitchen.
I might step outside for a minute.
I might get around to reading that book.
I might do all of the things I said I might do
yesterday.

Digitally Consumed

I pick you up to check again
for something that isn't there.
I know not much can change
since just a moment ago.
I need you and your validation,
but I always end up empty-handed.
You are a poisonous privilege
and a rapturous regret.
You ruin my life,
but I know I can't live without you.

Hello, Old Friend

Up from my bed, I rise.
My feet shuffle,
hesitant yet eager.
I feel the pit in my stomach.
My brain is infected with virulent curiosity.
I look at the ground.
I'm unsure whether I'm prepared to look up.
I do, anyway.
I'm overcome with emotions
all at one instant.
Every time I repeat this ritual,
I find myself facing a new girl.
She stares back at me,
and I don't recognize her.
She looks different from the last time.
I feel uncomfortable and uneasy
not knowing which version of her I'll see.
How can I recognize her
without knowing what she looks like?
I just want to know her
and love her unconditionally.
I can't keep meeting her like this.
It's inconsistent and disappointing.
I drag my feet back to my bed.
I curl up in my uncertainty
and let my tears carry me to sleep.
I awake with the pit and the curiosity once more.
I'm with her again.
Hello, old friend.

Please Don't Sea Me

I look at myself and feel too disgusted
to leave the house.
And then the disgust surges
when I acknowledge that terrible thought.
How could I think that way?
But how could I look this way?
I'm going to drown myself
in fabrics that hide me.
You may only see eyes
poking through my disguise.
You may see tears flow down,
but I won't tread in my self-inflicted sea.
I will let the current pull me in.
I'd rather drown in unseen depths
than show myself on the surface.

Pulp:

The soft, shapeless mass happening in the now,
not the fruit in its polished form or the aftermath
of digging in; the experiences: good, bad, and
in-between.

Hope of Hygieia

Here I stand
in all my womanly existence.
On the brink of the rest of my life.
Just now finding my footing.
Just now synchronizing my breath
with that of the world.

With my eyes full of sorrow
that an unripe fruit shouldn't know yet.
Head hanging like a pear tree
whose branches are growing weak.
Shoulders trying to stay firm,
trying to maintain some resilience.

But I'll let that slithering snake
wrap around my chest
and make its way to my generous hand
to take what little hope I have to offer.
And when it sheds its skin of yesterday,
I hope it takes my weary days, too.

So that I may ripen,
and my branches may reach for the sun.
So that I can breathe with the vigor
of all that surrounds me.
So my offerings are forever plentiful,
and I become her: Hygieia in all her health.

New Place

When I first moved to this city, the hot sting of
September pierced my skin,
and I wished only for the cold.
Now, the creeping autumn chill grazes my face to
say hello,
and I foresee sadness and comfort cuddled up
together.
Yellow leaves fall, and late summer fades away.
I look at my feet so often I have to notice the
leaves.
Squawking geese flock up from the water over the
bridge in the park.
They are leaving and starting a new chapter,
reaching for the above.
I am on the edge of everything and on the verge
of nothing.
Kicking stones on the street just to know I can
make things move;
to know I'm grounded, to know I'm here in nature
and life.
I'm chasing trains that never stop and waiting for
ones that never come.
And when I finally board, I want to let go and
allow myself to stumble
just to feel something.
Because falling is a distinct pain, a pinpointed
emotion.
Unlike this indescribable melancholy.

Word Vomit

For the first time in my life
I feel like throwing up
all the time.
I want to speak,
but instead of the usual
word vomit,
it's just the latter.
But maybe the nausea
is worth it,
so I stop opening
my big mouth.
Perhaps I can stay nauseous
and quiet
forever.

Until

I can't shake this nauseous feeling,
and I think the world is ending,
mind might be exaggerating,
but I feel this weight still.

I find my happiness is fleeting.
I really thought this thing had meaning.
I never thought of friendship leaving,
until it did, until.

I'm better now; my smile is gleaming,
but here I find myself still thinking
of memories and lots of laughing.
Now, I swallow the bitter pill.

Technicolor

I'm the sunshine
in your dark little life.
I'm the symmetry
in the sadness.
I'm a kaleidoscope of color
in your mysterious shades.
You're black and white,
but I'm technicolor.
I've got the hues you cannot see.

Trickle in My Heart

Trickle in my heart,
lingering little ache.

Yearning for it to start,
wondering if it's too late.

Forever intertwined,
perpetual hanging on.

What sparked so long ago,
I don't think is gone.

Reflecting

Our future is a reflection
on a shiny bathroom stall.
It's not a crystal clear view,
but I can still see it all.

It's like bright neon lights
shining on wet concrete.
The blurred hues melt,
but the image is still complete.

I wonder if it's pointless
to have held on for so long.
But each time you come back,
I prove the skeptics wrong.

It's been a while, and nothing's come
of the dream inside my head.
But you're getting better, and I can't
put my hopes for you to bed.

I'd sail across a stormy sea
if you'd greet me at the end.
If you asked to see me now,
through space and time, I'd bend.

Green Fingers

I put on cheap rings that will turn my fingers
green,
and I keep coming back when I know you'll just
leave.
Sometimes, I know better and still do dumb
things,
like trusting crappy boys and putting on crappy
rings.

Somewhat Strangers

We're somewhat strangers,
forgotten friends,
long-lost lovers.
All we have are memories
and your empty promises
to make more.
I wish I could forget you,
but unfinished things
bother me so.
How could I move on
from something that
never had the chance to end?
It paused inexplicably
right when things almost got good,
just like it did many times before.
Everything was left open-ended.
So, how could a curious mind
like mine not question,
not be tortured by what-ifs,
not ponder inconclusive halts,
not search for explanations?

Penny Toss

You toss me like a penny into water
and fish me out again when you feel like being
rich.
When your other distractions dry up.
When you remember
I'm still there waiting,
drowning in familiar waters,
sinking to the same depths,
hoping to see your hand above the surface
reaching to grab me again.
When you toss me, you don't wish for me.
You wish for me to be around still when you
decide I'm worthy again.

Juice:

The messy stuff that drips out after biting into pulp; how the sticky situations made me feel.

Nectarine Nonsense

My youth is nectarine nonsense,
juicy bites of pompous pulp,
ravenous ripping of spontaneous skin,
until I get to the hard pit in the center,
and my fun is over.
No more fruit to savor.
The sweetest thing I'll never taste again.

Sweet Life

I wish I could be alone forever
and only speak to strangers.
Keep thinking I've met my people,
but they never really fit.
I've lost my sense of self.
I don't like who I am
or who I've been pretending to be.
I'm not sure what I want,
but it's not this.
This can't be all.
Life can't be walking on eggshells.
Life has to be sweeter than this.
Please.
Please let it be sweeter.

Wolf in Sheep's Clothing

Your arcadian facade
blinded me from the truth.
I didn't recognize you,
wolf in sheep's clothing.

I thought you were a sheep.
Sheep from a quaint life.
Sheep with a good heart.
Sheep that can't do wrong.

You are not a sheep.

You are a wolf.
Wolf panting with privilege.
Wolf with a rotten soul.
Wolf that can't accept he's wrong.

What a cunning scheme
I fell for so easily,
because I am a sheep.
Sheep with a strong mind,
but still a sheep,
assuming the best,
hoping everyone
is a sheep, too.

You permeated the herd
with your sneaky tactics,
calculated moves,
bad intentions.
With no responsibility.

Please leave my pasture.
Leave my land to rest.
Wolves don't belong here.
My land is for sheep.

Canyon Collapse

I wish the deep canyons under my eyes
would keep eroding into my skull
until my body caves in.
No more dealing with anything
if I'm all warped inside myself.
Final collapse.
Thank God.

Thought Wrong

Thought I'd be exercising my mind,
but I've just been rubbing my temples.

Thought I'd be getting my hands dirty,
but I've just been holding up my heavy head.

Thought I'd found my perfect place,
but I've found myself out of place.

Thought the path would be straightforward,
but maybe I'm not on the right one.

I Left My Soul Down South

I fear no one will know me
like those people back home.
And I fear I won't see
those people for long.
I fear the big city will suck me in
when I want to travel home
like a tumbleweed in the wind.
The convulsive train
doesn't know my planted feet
like the stinging Texas concrete
knows my bare feet in July.
The tall buildings
are no wondrous sight
for my eyes
that have laid upon
wide open roads under a sorbet sky.
I don't care for the
Northeast disposition
like I thought I would.
And I'm always sick.
But I know that some
Southern twang
would soothe my throat
if I had anyone to
utter spontaneous sweetness to.
I always wanted to leave home
and go up North
because I thought big things
happen the higher you go.
But I think I left my soul down South,
and when I touched down in Dallas,

I let out the first breath of relief
that I've had in months.
And I always hated the heat.
I thought I could handle the
cold air,
but I didn't know there would be
other chills piercing my skin
besides the weather.
So now I might like some warmth back
from the golden sun
and the people who dance under it.
I think I might like to be back home.
I think I might miss what I was running from.

Mouthful

I have conversations stuck in my throat
that want to be had but never will.

I have words on the tip of my tongue
to scold you with the way they burn my mouth.

I have sentences to spew at you,
telling you what you did wrong so many times.

But I swallow my words and bite my tongue.
There's no use uttering a word to ears that won't
listen.

Love and War

Went looking for a great love,
all I found was a great war.
Always fighting for my life
just to get a bit more.

I thought I saw a raven in the tree,
but it was just a bag tangled up.
Just like I thought it was meant to be,
that you and I could be an us.

I thought I read the signals right
since you read them aloud to me,
but I had failed to notice
the other girls listening behind me.

You keep me in your pocket
when I'm convenient for your use,
but I'm tired of this waiting,
so love me or cut me loose.

I hold onto the potential
and cherish when you're here,
but every time I'm left alone
I face the truth that I fear.

I hate myself for knowing what's wrong
and doing it anyway.
I hate the way I won't give up
on this game I never wanted to play.

The saddest part of this turmoil
is that I know you'll never stay.
And though you'll never choose me,
I'll still choose you every day.

And now my heart is cracked
by the chisel in your hand
that shaped me into what you needed,
now lonely and broken, I stand.

Which Other Woman Am I

You like your girls blonde,
whether they're dirty or pure,
but I'm an auburn-haired enigma,
if you liked me, I wasn't sure.

You like girls in other states
and countries in the distance.
It's easy to leave someone on a screen
when you're afraid of commitment.

You told me about the others
as if expecting a reaction.
For a talkative girl, I sure turned quiet
when I realized I was a distraction.

You told me I was the only one
you could ever be yourself with.
That must have scared you badly,
so you left and chose to be selfish.

I never want to speak to you again,
though I've said that many times,
but I also want to scold you
for your silence and your crimes.

Revolving Door

You love to Irish exit through a revolving door,
don't know when you leave, but I know you'll be
back for more.
There were times I tried to catch you on your way
out,
but you left for the next stop on your romance
route.
I hoped like a fool for your inevitable return,
and I hate myself for that and the way that I
would yearn.
Naive and optimistic, I waited for you there,
thinking this time, when you came back, it would
all be fair.
But you never seemed to change, and my patience
grew thin,
got tired of the long game I knew I'd never win.

The distance between us
is no one's fault but yours.
That's just the way you want it,
entering and leaving doors.

Now, I return the favor
through the same revolving door.
I now have the power to leave,
I won't wait for you anymore.

Pit:

The core thoughts that connect me with humanity; realizations, big questions, and denouements.

Vase Value

If a vase had feelings,
would it hate how it was formed?
The way it curves and bends?
The way it is adorned?

Would it feel insecure
placed next to other vessels?
Even with flowers in its grasp,
would it still not feel special?

It's made to be displayed,
no matter how it's sculpted.
It's made to be a pretty thing,
not made to be insulted.

So, I picture myself as a vase,
a unique configuration,
a beautiful thing to look at,
not meant for self-degradation.

Questions, Questions

Am I living an illusion
through a third-person view?
Is my story already written,
or are my moments impromptu?

Can I ever grow up
and step into the ring of fire?
Can I stare into the face of menace
and accomplish what I desire?

Will my potential waste away
until I eventually burn out?
Will I ever amount to anything
like I had planned for my life route?

How can I part from my jaded thoughts
and cease to be a cynic?
How can I ever get unstuck
from this tiresome gimmick?

Hands, Deltas, and the World

Hands are deltas that connect rivers of love
and human connection.
They are innocent and scandalous.
They are supple and unyielding.
They are gentle and callous.
Hands have felt the world.
They indulge in its stories
and share them with those they touch.
Hands are connectors
and lovers
and storytellers.
Hands are but hands,
but hands are the world
and all of its deltas.

The Taste of Time

Everyone misses the old days
like they were even there.

The time's slipping away,
and we're suddenly aware.

Sweet nostalgia on my tongue.
I can taste the days gone by.

That flavor of life will fade.
I can't help but wonder why.

The Days

The days are sand slipping through my fingers,
raindrops racing on the window,
turning pages of a book.

The days are mundane,
drastically unimportant,
wasted on what-ifs.

The days pass by,
speeding like a train while I watch from afar,
fading like an old picture.

The days haunt me.
I feel them lurking behind every corner.
They hide under my bed and in my shadow.

The days are what I fear most:
a reminder of inevitable fate,
the limit of life.

Time Unveiling Truth

Father Time, that scoundrel of scandal,
pulls back the golden robes
of our blissful avoidance,
exposing the reality we try to hide from.
But we can't fight back
from down here.
And with arrows out of reach,
they look down on us,
wondering if we see it now.
Our love can never last.
Our bodies won't remain.
The things we love have to fade.
It's the cruel schedule of life,
and we must adhere to it.
We have this moment to grasp the truth
before Time takes her away.
Dark wings flying through the sun
and off to some distant place
where our ignorant love
can't exist.

That's Life

What's the point of making today count
if tomorrow's not guaranteed?

Life doesn't owe us an abundance of days
no matter how hard we may plead?

We know bad things will come to others
and expect good things to come our way.

But life's rotten touch spreads like mold.
We lose the game we're forced to play.

Everything is random, and nothing's ever fair.
You'll balance on the seesaw of glory and despair.

Transient Transportation

I like to think of moments past
on trains passing by
and ponder on people gone
on planes flying high.

Looking out the window
at blurred buildings and trees,
I picture what I wish was true,
or what I wish never left me.

Something about being alone
in a seat striding somewhere
makes me feel the weight of life
in my sunken, sullen stare.

My head pressed against the glass
makes it easier to think
about how one second they're there
then they're gone in a blink.

Though I have a destination,
I'm heading to the great unknown.
I'm moving through my world,
reaping the seeds I've sown.

My arrival is bittersweet,
but I know that I'll be fine.
I'll go make more moments
to remember in years down the line.

Wish of Life

I never pass a dandelion
that I don't greet with a gust.
I never let the clock pass 11:11
before I close my eyes and yearn.
I always catch fallen eyelashes
on my fingertips and let them fly.
I always spot angel numbers
and count my blessings.
Don't know if I believe in astrology,
but I'll listen with eager ears.
Can't quite believe in a god,
but I feel the universe on my shoulders.
Don't believe in meant-to-be,
nothing like fate or destiny,
but I do believe in connected souls
and invisible strings.
I'm not superstitious;
I've broken three mirrors, and I feel fine.
But sometimes, when I really want,
I cross my fingers for cherry-on-top luck.
I believe in love,
though I've never met it.
I believe one day, I will.
I think life is accidental;
I think it goes on,
for better or for worse.
But how splendid is it to be alive?
To want.
To wish.
To love.
To live.

Simple Pleasures

When it comes to death,
I don't fear the dying.
I fear missing out on the best parts of living:
lying on my carpet and staring at my bookshelf
and the posters on my walls,
going to see a movie by myself in an old theater,
laughing until my stomach hurts,
smelling the crisp air on an October day.
I don't know what happens after we die.
I don't think we can know.
Maybe life after death is so profound,
I won't feel so sad about what once was
and the things that once made me happy.
Or maybe life after death is nothing.
But I hope I can hold onto those things
in some way or another.
Maybe the simple pleasures live on in
consciousness.

About the Author

Nina Cairo is a writer, creative, and student at the University of Texas at Austin. In addition to being a poet, she is a collage maker, a frequent concert-goer, an avid cinema lover, and an aspiring traveler. She hopes to continue writing and creating projects.